Would You Rather Game Book For Kids, Teens And Adults

How to Play

First of all, you need at least two-three players.

Try asking questions of the whole group instead of simply asking one person. This may take more time, but you'll be able to compare different answers amongst the whole crowd or just gather different answers with different argumentation.
You may also want to set a time limit for making decisions. Thus the game will go faster and be more interesting, as players will be motivated by their instincts more, than thoughts.
You can use a gaming hourglass or set the timer to track the "thinking" time.
The shorter that is the more pressure participants will get to answer.
You can play until you have creative ideas or until someone won't be able to make a choice.
Watching them trying to find the solution will be hilarious!

Have a nice game!

Would You Rather...?

Would you rather...

Eat an egg with a chicken inside
or
eat five cooked cockroaches?

Be friends with a tamed polar bear
or
a tamed cobra?

Would you rather....

Have an extremely smart talking parrot
or
a flying pony?

Live on Mars
or
continue to live on
Earth in the future?

Would you rather...

Have hair
all over your body
or
have purple skin?

Know everything
or
have the power
to do anything?

Would you rather...

Be a genius
scientist
or
a genius
poet/artist?

Be able to heal
any disease
or
be able to bring
the dead back to life?

Would you rather...

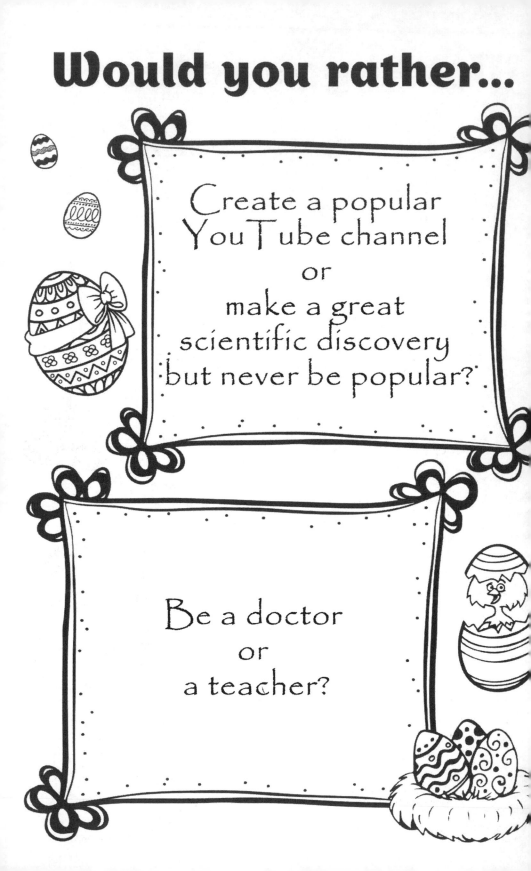

Create a popular YouTube channel
or
make a great scientific discovery but never be popular?

Be a doctor
or
a teacher?

Would you rathe....

Be a dreamer with
a wild imagination
or
a doer who doesn't
think creatively?

Be 5 years older
or
seven years younger?

Would you rather...

Have a hairy tongue or have your nose where your belly button is?

Eat vanilla ice cream with pickled herring or drink a glass of fish oil?

Would you rather...

Have a
penguin
or
a cheetah
for a pet?

Be able only
to listen to others
or
be able only to say
something to others?

Would you rather...

Drink an elixir of life
or
have a Philosopher's

Be Cinderella
or
Sleeping beauty?

Would you rather....

Travel all around
the world
or
travel in outer space?

Be able to bring back
extinct species
or
be able to stop the
extinction of species
that exist now?

Would you rather...

Be the most beautiful
and smartest person
or
the richest and most
powerful person
in the world?

Have a
talking cat
or
be able to understand
what all dogs
are thinking?

Would you rather...

Lose your
sense of smell
or
your sense
of taste?

Be a single child
or
have many siblings?

Would you rather...

Be great at math
or
an amazing writer?

Have a
billion dollars
or
be able to live
up to 500 years?

Would you rather...

See an alien
or
see a ghost?

Create a perfect robot
similar to a human
or
teach all animals
human language?

Would you rather...

Get up at 3 a.m.
or
at 1 p.m. for the
rest of your life?

Fall in love
at first sight
or
gradually develop
feelings for a friend?

Would you rather...

Ask silly questions
or
answer them?

See a meteorite fall
or
see a double rainbow?

Would you rather...

Drink hot chocolate
in the summer
or
eat ice cream
in the winter.

Be able to live
without oxygen
or
without food?

Would you rather...

Live in
Ancient Greece
or
in 25th century?

Be able to turn
anything into gold
or
into food?

Would you rather...

Be able to do
complex calculations
in your head
or
to play any song
after listening
to it once?

Bring to life
your dead relatives
or
see your family
members from
the future?

Would you rather...

Be a very kind-hearted
but a stupid person
or
be an extremely
intelligent evil person?

Be a president
of the country
or
be the first human
to live on Mars?

Would you rather...

Be a butterfly that lives several days
or
a snail that lives 100 years?

Go to Disneyland whenever you want for free
or
eat ice cream whenever you want for free?

Would you rather...

Be a movie star
or
a first astronaut
in the world?

Have only friends
who are much older
than you
or
friends who are
much younger
than you?

Would you rather...

Fall asleep
for a year
or
have insomnia
for a year?

Be able to read
people's minds
or
speak 10 foreign
languages?

Would you rathe....

Be a lazy person
with big talent
or
a hard-working person
who doesn't have
any special talents?

Live at the treehouse
or
at the house
under the water?

Would you rather...

Never age
or
be unable
to remember
the past day?

Climb Mount Everest
or
be at the bottom
of the ocean?

Would you rather...

Never have wrinkles
or
never be able
to smile?

Be Harry Potter
or
Hermione Granger?

Would you rather...

Have a look at
an extinct animal
or
an animal that
would live a million
years from now?

Live in the house
of your dreams
or
in the country
of your dreams?

Would you rather...

Bring back
a dinosaurs
or
mammoths
from extinction?

Be friends with
someone who
never laughs
or
with someone who
never makes
you laugh?

Would you rather...

Be the best dancer
as long as nobody
could see you dance
or
be an average dancer
who can perform
for anybody?

Have a talking dog
or
a talking cat?

Would you rathe....

Be a Yogi
or
an acrobatic
performer?

Make a magic potion
that could make
someone tell only truth
or
make someone wiser?

Would you rather...

Relive your
childhood
or
your teenage years?

Apologize for
something you
didn't commit
or
really hurt someone
and never apologize
for it?

Would you rathe...

Be alone
at Christmas
or
on Valentine's Day?

Taste a hybrid of
mango and onion
or
a hybrid of
lemon and peach?

Would you rather...

Save 5 strangers
or
1 loved one
from death?

Be rich
but have no talents
or
be exceptionally gifted.
but have no money?

Would you rather...

Eat a spoonful
of wasabi
or
a spoonful of
Tabasco sauce?

Be yourself
or
somebody else?

Would you rather...

Have a
private airplane
or
a cruise ship?

Win 1 million dollars
in a lottery
or
meet the love
of your life tomorrow?

Would you rather...

Be in the room
full of baby pandas
or
baby koalas?

Go to the circus with
holographic animals
performing tricks
or
the real animals?

Would you rather...

Have allergies
to strawberries
or
chocolate?

Live in a
haunted house
or
live in a house
with a poltergeist?

Would you rathe....

Eat any food
you like for the
rest of your life
or
eat one pill a day
instead of food for
the rest of your life?

Be a mad scientist
or
a mad artist?

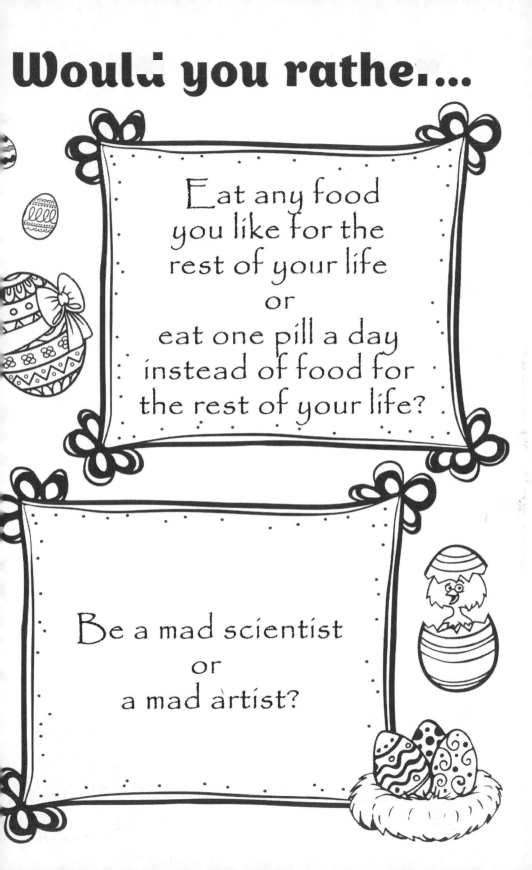

Would you rather...

Save polar bears
from extinction
or
pandas?

Live on an
uninhabited island
or
live in a society
but be deaf and mute?

Would you rather...

Have one life
or
reincarnate
again and again?

Be able to turn
invisible at will
or
to turn into
any animal at will?

Would you rather...

Have many
extroverted friends
or
have two
introverted ones?

Never love
or
never be loved?

Would you rather...

Be friends
with Elon Musk
or
Homer Simpson?

Live with
someone you hate
or
live completely alone?

Would you rather...

Have super long hair which you can't cut
or
have no hair at all?

Be a king
or
a president?

Would you rather...

Eat sweets
or
fruits?

Smell an old fish
or
find a dead rat?

Would you rather...

Only be able
to whisper
or
only be able
to shout?

Be a
Buddhist monk
or
be a beautiful
fluffy cat that lived
in a loving home?

Would you rather...

Eat a whole plate
of fried spiders
or
eat a jar of
pickled snakes?

Be immortal
or
have an unlimited
amount of money?

Would you rather...

Be a crazy person whom people believe to be a normal one

or

a normal person but who is perceived as crazy by everybody?

Be the most beautiful person on the planet

or

the healthiest one?

Would you rather...

Have a very long
and boring life
or
a short one with
lots of interesting
experiences?

Have a
settled schedule
or
change your plans
five times a day?

Would you rather...

Be an
ambulance driver
or
take part in
Formula 1?

Be the best chess
player in the world
or
develop artificial
intelligence that could
beat even the world's
greatest chess player?

Would you rather...

Meet a Jinn
and have three of
your wishes granted
or
be a Jinn who could
grant any wishes
but his own?

Have a lot of likes
for posting
a stupid joke
or
a few likes
for posting
a wise quote?

Would you rather...

Be a vegetarian
or
eat only exotic
types of meat
(ex crocodile meat,
snake meat,
shark meat, etc)?

Never know your
real name
or
never know what
you really look like?

Would you rathe....

Have a big head
or
a long neck?

Be on the cover
of a fashion magazine
or
play a cameo
appearance on your
favorite TV show?

Would you rather...

Be afraid of losing
your loved one
or
losing yourself?

Have a big
or
a small wedding?

Would you rather...

Sing in opera
or
in a hard rock band?

Have
celebrity parents
or
celebrity friends?

Would you rather...

Give up your
smartphone for the
rest of your life
or
give up your
favorite food?

Be able
to fly like a hawk
or
swim like a shark?

Would you rather...

Have an eye
on your forehead
or
seven fingers
on the left hand?

Be an angel
or
a fairy?

Would you rather...

Be bald
or
have an extremely
hairy body?

Drink a bottle
of seawater
or
one cup sour milk?

Would you rather...

Be God
for one day
or
an angel
for one year?

Change
your eye color
or
your hair color?

Would you rather...

Have an extremely
good intuition
or
x-ray vision?

Live in Australia
or
in France?

Would you rather...

Be a superhero
or
a magic wizard?

It be Christmas
every day
or
it be Easter
every day?

Would you rather...

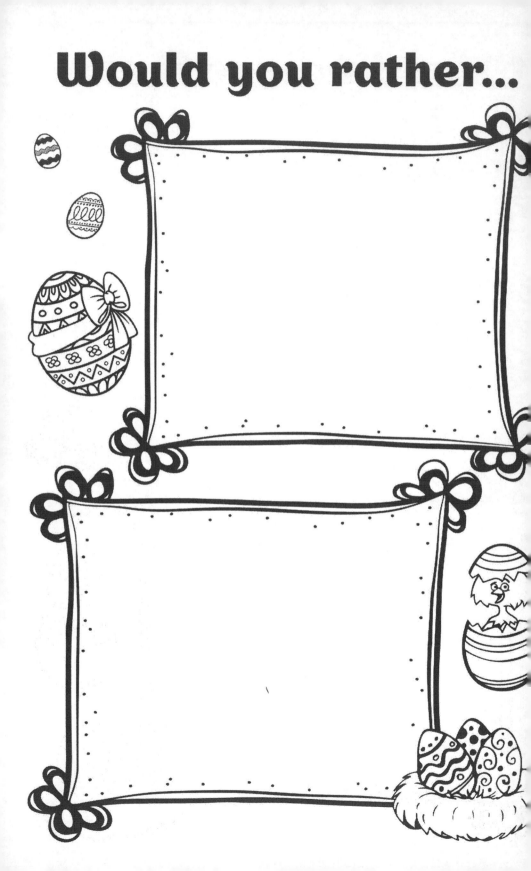

Would you rather...

Would you rather...

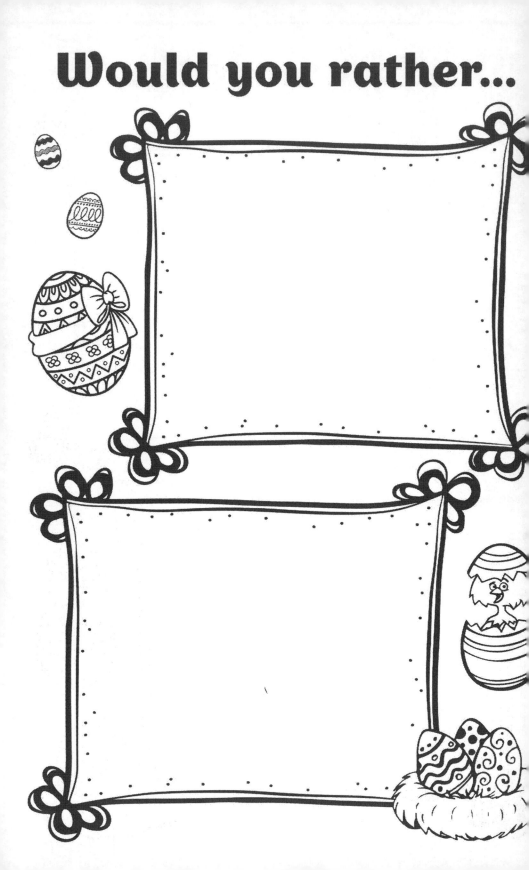

Would you rathe....

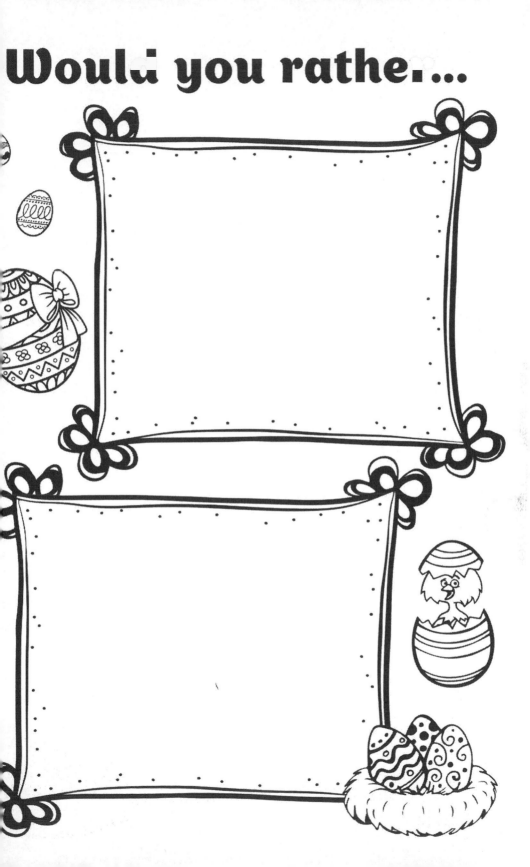

Trivia Questions
&
Answers

Trivia Questions & Answers

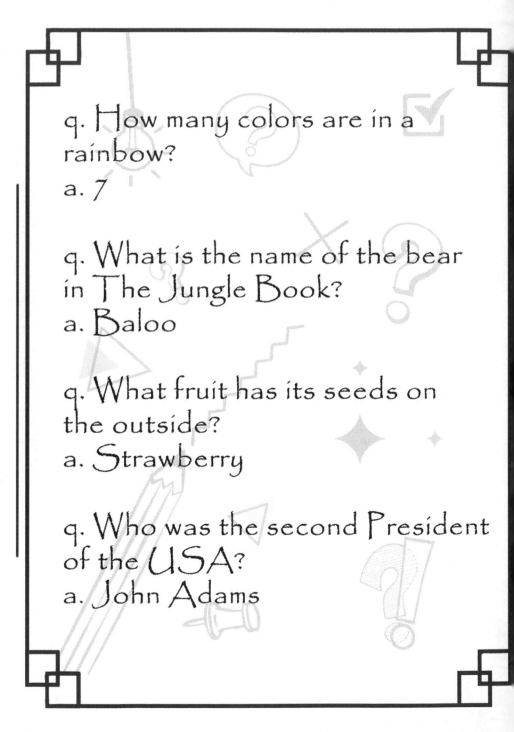

q. How many colors are in a rainbow?
a. 7

q. What is the name of the bear in The Jungle Book?
a. Baloo

q. What fruit has its seeds on the outside?
a. Strawberry

q. Who was the second President of the USA?
a. John Adams

Trivia Questions & Answers

q. What is the largest jungle in the world?
a. Amazon Rainforest

q. What's the name of the galaxy Earth is located in?
a. The Milky Way

q. What's the longest river in the United States?
a. The Mississippi.

q. What is the biggest desert in the world?
a. Sahara

Trivia Questions & Answers

q. How many inches are there in a yard?
a. 36

q. How many legs does a spider have?
a. 8

q. Name the school that Harry Potter attended?
a. Hogwarts

q. Saint Patrick is the Patron Saint of which country?
a. Ireland

Trivia Questions & Answers

q. How many years are there in a millennium?
a. 1000

q. What color is Smurfs?
a. Blue

q. Which planet in our Solar System is known for having a ring?
a. Saturn

q. How many days are there in April?
a. 30

Trivia Questions & Answers

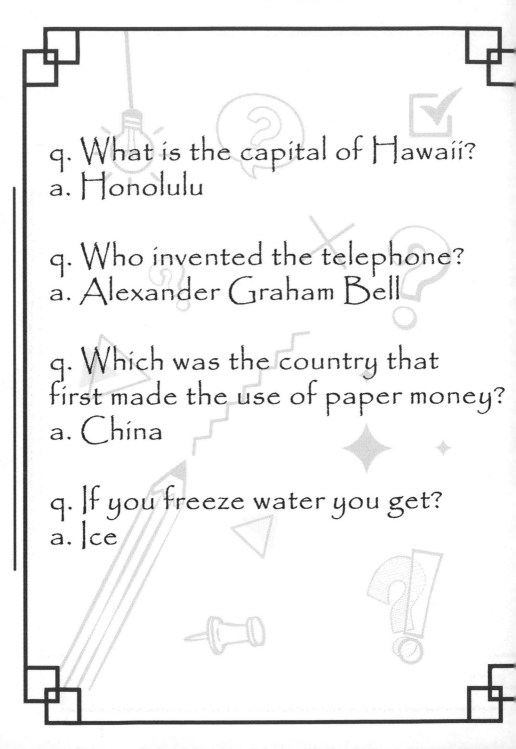

q. What is the capital of Hawaii?
a. Honolulu

q. Who invented the telephone?
a. Alexander Graham Bell

q. Which was the country that first made the use of paper money?
a. China

q. If you freeze water you get?
a. Ice

Trivia Questions & Answers

q. Pharaoh is the title given to the rulers of which ancient country?
a. Egypt

q. What country has a maple leaf on their national flag?
a. Canada

q. Name the largest animal in the world?
a. Elephant

q. What is the name of the largest ocean on earth?
a. The Pacific Ocean

Trivia Questions & Answers

q. How many pairs of wings does a bee have?
a. Two

q. Who was Abu in Aladin?
a. A monkey

q. How many rings Olympic logo have?
Five

q. Who wrote Oliver Twist?
a. Charles Dickens

Trivia Questions & Answers

q. How many days are in a leap year?
a. 365

q. From what tree do acorns come?
a. Oak

q. Which is the biggest spider in the world?
a. Tarantula

q. Which is the highest mountain in Africa?
a. Mount Kilimanjaro

Trivia Questions & Answers

q. How many planets are in our solar system?
a. Eight Planets

q. Which is the smallest country in the world?
a. Vatican

q. Name the tallest animal in the world?
a. Giraffe

q. What is another name for a tidal wave?
a. Tsunami

Trivia Questions & Answers

q. What is the most popular dog breed found in the USA?
a. The Labrador Retriever

q. The scientific study of plant life is known as what?
a. Botany

q. Where did the Olympic Games originate?
a. Greece

q. Which came first, the Jurassic or Cretaceous Period?
a. The Jurassic Period

Trivia Questions & Answers

q. How many sides does a hexagon have?
a. Six

q. What is the name of the highest mountain on earth?
a. Mount Everest

q. Solar power generates electricity from what source?
a. The Sun

q. What part of the human body contains five metacarpal bones?
a. The hand

Trivia Questions & Answers

q. What are the only two countries in South America that do not border Brazil?
a. Chile and Ecuador

q. Which fictional city is the home of Batman?
a. Gotham City

q. Babe Ruth is associated with which sport?
a. Baseball

q. What kind of magic is used for evil purposes?
a. Black magic

Trivia Questions & Answers

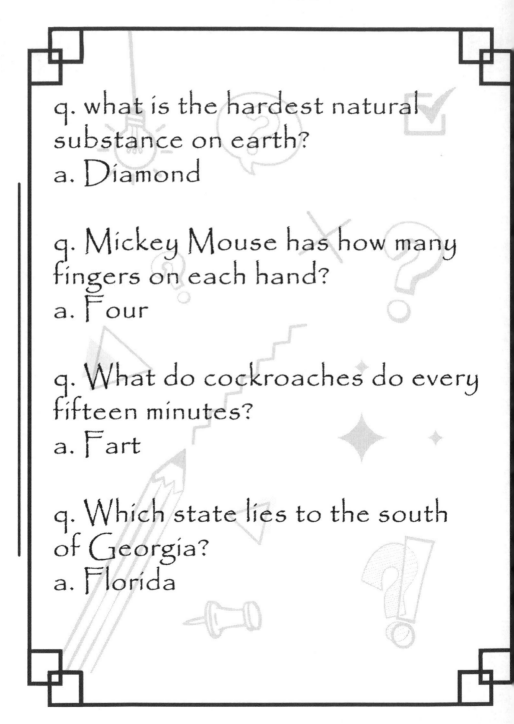

q. what is the hardest natural substance on earth?
a. Diamond

q. Mickey Mouse has how many fingers on each hand?
a. Four

q. What do cockroaches do every fifteen minutes?
a. Fart

q. Which state lies to the south of Georgia?
a. Florida

If your kids have enjoyed this book, please consider leaving a short review on the book Amazon page.
It will help others to make an informed decision before buying my book.

Regards,
Robert B. Grand

Made in the USA
San Bernardino, CA
10 April 2020